Ela A  SO-ADV-903

275 Mohawk Trail,

(847) 438-3433

www.eapl.org

31241009349369

DEC - - 2018

YOUNG SPORTS GREATS

BRYCE HARPER

PHIL CORSO

PowerKiDS
press.

New York

Published in 2019 by The Rosen Publishing Group, Inc.
29 East 21st Street, New York, NY 10010

First Edition

Editor: Elizabeth Krajnik
Book Design: Michael Flynn

Photo Credits: Cover, p. 1 Rich Schultz/Getty Images; pp. 4–8, 10, 12–14, 16–18, 20, 22–23 (background) Eo naya/Shutterstock.com; p. 4 KonstantinChristian/Shutterstock.com; pp. 5, 7, 9, 11, 13, 15, 21 Icon Sports Wire/Icon Sportswire/Getty Images; p. 6 Elsa/Getty Images Sport/Getty Images; p. 14 Mega Pixel/Shutterstock.com; p. 17 MCT/Tribune News Service/Getty Images; p. 18 StefanoT/Shutterstock.com; p. 19 The Washington Post/Getty Images; p. 22 Chris Troutman/Getty Images Sport/Getty Images.

Cataloging-in-Publication Data

Title: Bryce Harper / Phil Corso.
Description: New York : PowerKids Press, 2019. | Series: Young sports greats | Includes glossary and index.
Identifiers: LCCN ISBN 9781538330296 (pbk.) | ISBN 9781538330272 (library bound) | ISBN 9781538330302 (6 pack)
Subjects: LCSH: Harper, Bryce, 1992–Juvenile literature. | Baseball players–United States–Biography–Juvenile literature.
Classification: LCC GV865.H268 C67 2019 | DDC 796.357092 B–dc23

Manufactured in the United States of America

CPSIA Compliance Information: Batch #CS18PK For Further Information contact Rosen Publishing, New York, New York at 1-800-237-9932

CONTENTS

HITTING THE T AT 3 4

A FAMILY AFFAIR 6

PLAYING UP 8

A LASTING IMPRESSION 10

BYE SCHOOL 12

HANDLING THE HYPE . . 14

DRAFTING HISTORY 16

THE SLUMP 18

THE BRYCE IS RIGHT . . . 20

SHARPER HARPER 22

GLOSSARY 23

INDEX 24

WEBSITES 24

HITTING THE T AT 3

In 1995, when Bryce Harper was just three years old, he stepped up to bat at his very first T-ball game in his hometown of Las Vegas, Nevada. Just 14 years later, Harper was on the June 8, 2009, cover of *Sports Illustrated* as "baseball's chosen one." Surrounded by hype, fans and **scouts** waited to see which Major League Baseball (MLB) team would select him in the entry **draft**.

Like other young, hardworking professional athletes, Harper had to put in long hours and be ambitious to become a professional athlete at such a young age.

SPORTS CORNER

The average lifespan of a major league baseball is anywhere between five and seven pitches. A typical baseball game will go through roughly 70 balls on average.

AS A YOUNG MAN, ONE OF HARPER'S GOALS WAS TO BE IN THE HALL OF FAME.

A FAMILY AFFAIR

Family played a big role in Bryce Harper's baseball beginnings. He got his start in baseball tossing the ball around with his brother Bryan, who is three years older than him. Playing with his older sibling forced Bryce to **hone** his skills quickly.

ONE OF HARPER'S FORMER TEAMMATES SAID, "I'VE NEVER SEEN SOMEONE HIT SO MUCH WITH HIS DAD."

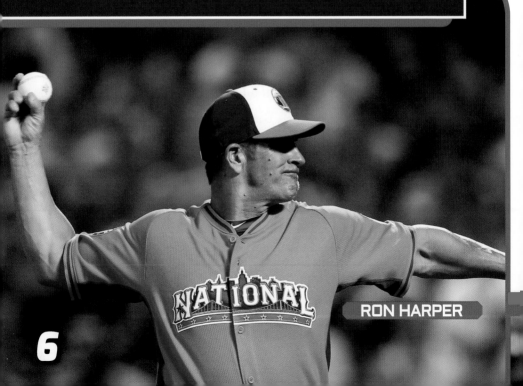

RON HARPER

BRYCE HARPER

BRYAN HARPER

Both Bryan and Bryce practiced with their father Ron Harper, who worked with his sons on their hitting and throwing. To help the boys become better players, he used to pitch them small things such as sunflower seeds, bottle tops, and dried red beans. He took them to tournaments, batting cages, clinics in California, and practiced with them in the backyard.

PLAYING UP

From the first time he picked up a baseball bat, Harper played baseball with older kids. By the time he was playing travel baseball in his early teens, Harper became known as the "best kid out there" even though he was two or three years younger than most of his teammates. His hard work and natural athleticism helped set him apart.

Harper and his batting power helped lead his earliest travel teams to national championships abroad. Before reaching high school, Harper was named to several All-American Teams and was Player of the Year playing travel ball in 2007.

SPORTS CORNER

In 1903, the Boston Americans were the first team to ever win the MLB World Series. The team later became known as the Boston Red Sox.

HARPER WAS USED TO BEING IN THE SPOTLIGHT AT A YOUNG AGE BECAUSE OF HIS ABILITY TO KEEP UP WITH OLDER PLAYERS.

A LASTING IMPRESSION

By the time Harper reached high school, in the position of catcher, he was already a known heavy hitter and future pro. As a **sophomore** at Las Vegas High School, he averaged about 1.6 hits per game and was on base nearly 70 percent of the time.

Harper and his incredible batting average turned heads in the sports world. Scouts guessed he'd be selected first overall in the MLB entry draft three years down the road. However, these promising guesses didn't stop him from working hard. During the remainder of his short high school career, Harper put in extra hours practicing his hitting to give him an advantage.

BRYCE HARPER'S SOPHOMORE YEAR STATS

GAMES	BATTING AVERAGE	ON BASE PERCENTAGE	HITS	RBIs	RUNS
23	.569	.689	37	26	37

IN 2009, HARPER WAS RANKED 1,381 NATIONALLY AND 14TH IN NEVADA FOR VARSITY BASEBALL PLAYERS.

BYE SCHOOL

Harper's **amateur** baseball career was short lived. He and his father decided that he would drop out of high school and pursue a professional career playing baseball.

At the end of his sophomore year, Harper passed his General Educational Development exam, earning him the equivalent of a high school diploma. He was then eligible for the 2010 amateur draft and to play professional baseball.

Harper quickly enrolled at the College of Southern Nevada. He was just 16 years old. Later that year, his brother Bryan transferred from Cal State Northridge to play with him on the baseball team.

SPORTS CORNER

When he was a sophomore, Harper hit a 502-foot (153 m) home run at Tampa Bay's Tropicana Field. During his freshman year, he hit a 570-foot (174 m) home run that flew over five lanes of traffic.

WHEN HARPER JOINED THE COLLEGE OF SOUTHERN NEVADA'S BASEBALL TEAM, HE HAD HIGH HOPES FOR THE 2010 AMATEUR DRAFT, WHERE HE WAS EXPECTED TO BE ONE OF THE FIRST PICKS FROM A TOP TEAM.

HANDLING THE HYPE

Harper handled the pressure of being a draft prospect very well. In college, he broke school and league records, raking in numbers such as 29 home runs, 89 RBIs, a .442 batting average, and stealing 18 bases in 62 games.

In 2009, Harper was named Baseball America's high school player of the year and player of the year in his conference the following season. In 2010, the same year as the big draft, he received the Golden Spikes Award, which is awarded to the country's best amateur player each year.

AT JUST 17 YEARS OLD, HARPER WAS EXPECTED TO BE THE FIRST PICK IN THE MLB DRAFT.

DRAFTING HISTORY

After years of hard work, the Washington Nationals picked 17-year-old Harper first overall in the 2010 First-Year Player Draft. Harper is the first junior college player to ever be selected first in the draft.

Soon after being drafted, Harper and the Nationals signed a five-year contract worth $9.9 million, including a $6.25 million signing bonus, and eight **semesters** of college tuition.

Even though Harper played catcher for much of his early career, the Nationals put him in the outfield to prepare him for the major leagues and also to make sure he didn't become injured.

SPORTS CORNER

Some studies have shown that catchers often suffer injuries to their knees from squatting in position. These injuries never go away, and may cause pain for the rest of the person's life.

ON AUGUST 26, 2010, THE WASHINGTON NATIONALS ANNOUNCED HARPER WOULD BE THEIR FIRST PICK IN THE 2010 FIRST-YEAR PLAYER DRAFT.

17

THE SLUMP

Shortly after being drafted, Harper began playing for the Nationals' minor league baseball **affiliate** the Hagerstown Suns. However, Harper's numbers weren't as good as some people expected. Following an eye exam and a new set of contact lenses, though, Harper's numbers began improving. The team's **optometrist** told Bryce that he had some of the worst eyes he's ever seen! The contact lenses greatly improved Bryce's game.

Harper worked his way up to the Nationals' Triple-A affiliate team in Syracuse, New York, before being called up to the major leagues in April 2012 to fill in for an injured player. After that season's All-Star Game, Harper's numbers started declining. He struggled in the batter's box and showed frustration on the field.

HARPER WON THE 2012 NATIONAL LEAGUE **ROOKIE** OF THE YEAR AWARD.

MINOR LEAGUE TOTALS (2011)

GAMES	AT BATS	RUNS	HITS	HOME RUNS	RBIs	BATTING AVERAGE
109	387	63	115	17	58	.297

THE BRYCE IS RIGHT

Even though Harper's first season in the major leagues had its share of ups and downs, he was named one of the National League's Final Vote **candidates** for the 2012 All-Star Game. Harper finished third in the voting, but made it onto the roster with two other Nationals teammates and was the youngest position player to make an All-Star roster.

By the end of his first season with the Nationals, Harper's stats picked up dramatically and helped the team reach the playoffs. Harper hit his first season home run in the National League Division Series against the St. Louis Cardinals from October 7 to October 12, 2012.

SPORTS CORNER

Harper's first game as a stand-in player for the Nationals' Ryan Zimmerman was against the L.A. Dodgers on April 28, 2012.

HARPER HELPED THE WASHINGTON NATIONALS GET TO THE PLAYOFFS IN THE 2017 SEASON. THE TEAM PLAYED THE CHICAGO CUBS IN THE NATIONAL LEAGUE DIVISION SERIES.

MAJOR LEAGUE TOTALS (ROOKIE SEASON)

GAMES	AT BATS	RUNS	HITS	HOME RUNS	RBIs	BATTING AVERAGE
139	553	98	144	22	59	.270

SHARPER HARPER

Every season since his rookie year, Bryce Harper has earned himself a reputation for being Mr. Clutch. He comes in with big hits when the Nationals need them the most. On April 18, 2015, he hit the longest home run of his pro career so far—461 feet (141 m)—against the Philadelphia Phillies.

On May 13, 2017, Harper agreed to a one-year $21.625 million contract with the Nationals for 2018. That salary is a record for any major league player who has less than six years of playing at the major-league level. That night, he hit a game-winning home run as his way of saying thank you.

GLOSSARY

affiliate: An organization that is a member of a larger organization.

amateur: A person who takes part in sports for fun and not for pay.

candidate: A person who is being considered for a position.

draft: The practice of choosing someone to play on a professional sports team.

hone: To sharpen or improve upon one's skills.

optometrist: An eye doctor.

rookie: A first-year player in a professional sport.

scout: Someone who searches for talented young athletes in the hope of recruiting them.

semester: One of two terms that make up a school year.

sophomore: A student in the second year of high school or college.

INDEX

A

All-Star Game, 18

B

Boston Americans, 8
Boston Red Sox, 8

C

Cal State Northridge, 12
College of Southern Nevada, 12

D

draft, 4, 10, 13, 14, 15, 16, 17, 18

G

Golden Spikes Award, 14

H

Harper, Bryan, 6, 7, 12
Harper, Ron, 7

L

L.A. Dodgers, 20

M

Major League Baseball, 10, 16, 20

N

National League, 19, 20, 21

P

Philadelphia Phillies, 22
Player of the Year, 8

R

Rookie of the Year, 19

S

Sports Illustrated, 4
St. Louis Cardinals, 20

W

Washington Nationals, 16, 17, 18, 20, 21, 22
World Series, 8

WEBSITES

Due to the changing nature of Internet links, PowerKids Press has developed an online list of websites related to the subject of this book. This site is updated regularly. Please use this link to access the list: www.powerkidslinks.com/ysg/harper